Bay Boys **3**

Adrian Goes Out There!

DAVID METZENTHEN

Illustrated by Michelle Ker

Triple**3**Play

 sundance

Published by
Sundance Publishing
P.O. Box 1326
234 Taylor Street
Littleton, MA 01460

Copyright © text David Metzenthen 1999
Copyright © illustrations Michelle Ker 1999

First published 1999 as Supa Dazzlers by
Addison Wesley Longman Australia Pty Limited
95 Coventry Street
South Melbourne 3205 Australia
Exclusive United States Distribution: Sundance Publishing

ISBN 0-7608-4794-0

Printed in Canada

Contents

Chapter 1

The Great Outdoors

I stay out in the surf all Sunday morning. I stay out in the surf all Sunday afternoon.

I spend nearly all Sunday in the water, because next week I won't be able to surf at all. Next week I'll be at Camp Rolling River, an outdoor camp that some of us from school are going to. So today Adrian Swift catches as many waves as he can, and then he sadly puts his board to bed.

Next, I pack my backpack and wonder what lies ahead for the thirty of us from Blue Water Bay School. Outdoor camps are supposed to be character-building. Outdoor camps are supposed to improve teamwork. Outdoor camps are supposed to make leaders of us. It says so in the letter right here.

That seems like an awful lot to achieve in five days.

We set off for Camp Rolling River in a silver bus. I sit in the backseat with my friends, Moppsy, Marco-man, Phil, and Aysha. We're all happier than usual because we're going off to camp, and we're missing a week of school.

"The great outdoors!" says Moppsy. "I'm going to climb cliffs and swim rivers. Ms. Radcliff will think I'm a real action hero."

Ms. Radcliff is my special math teacher. Moppsy wants to impress her. Well, Moppsy wants to impress everyone. Ms. Radcliff is our leader for the week. I must say, I don't think she's the luckiest person in the world. We aren't exactly the *A-Team*. And it's easy to see why. Look at our feet.

None of us even have hiking boots. We're all wearing sneakers, apart from Marco, who's wearing rubber thongs.

Camp Rolling River is set by an inlet where a river meets the sea. There's plenty of calm water to swim in and paddle canoes in, and there are lots of trees.

"Wilderness!" says Marco as he puts down his backpack in front of our old, green, wooden hut. "Let me at it!"

"Hey," says Phil, pointing. "Check out the obstacle course."

I can see rope nets, cable bridges, a wall of logs, things to crawl over, and things to crawl under. "Somehow," I say, "I can't see Ms. Radcliff breaking any world records on that stuff."

"Oh, I don't know," says Moppsy. "Maybe once she lets her hair down, she might be an outdoors superstar."

9

Ms. Radcliff has red hair that she coils on the top of her head. She wears glasses, too. She's not my idea of what an outdoors superstar looks like—but then I've been known to be wrong once or twenty times before.

The Screaming Parrots

The first thing we have to do in our group of five is to think up a name for ourselves. This is to develop teamwork, I think.

"The Destroyers," suggests Moppsy.

"Maybe not," says Ms. Radcliff, who is wearing a thick, pink sweater. She doesn't seem to have any hiking boots, either. She's wearing plain sneakers—no stripes, no stars, no colors, no pump-up tongues, and no sponge cushioning. I like them!

"How about the Nerd Birds?" I say.

"That's nice," says Aysha, "but how about the Tree Troopers? We're here, way out in the sticks."

"Sounds a bit too vegetable," says Phil. "How about the Screaming Sea Eagles?"

"How about the Screaming Parrots," suggests Marco, "from South America?"

Ms. Radcliff nods.

"I like the Screaming Parrots part," she says, "but I think we should forget the South America bit."

I look at Moppsy, and he looks at me. We laugh. Ms. Radcliff is radical!

"The Screaming Parrots it is then," says Mopps. "*Fantastic!*"

Chapter 3

Obstacles Everywhere

The second thing the Screaming Parrots have to do as a team is the obstacle course. We each have to do one lap, with two Screaming Parrots on either side in case we fall. It's not a race or anything.

Moppsy looks at the course, which is set in and around big trees. "This *will* be character-building," he says.

"Not if you break your arm it won't be," says Marco.

I study the various rope and cable bridges. I check out the log walls and balancing pole. I look at the crawling test. "We can do this stuff," I say. "No problem!"

Aysha elbows Moppsy. "That's leadership for you. The Screaming Parrots are doing really well already."

Ms. Radcliff looks at the bridges, walls, and logs.

"I have about as good a sense of balance as an egg," she says. "To tell you the truth, kids, I'm worried about this."

Marco-man gives Ms. Radcliff his Number One smile. "You'll be OK, Ms. Radcliff. We won't let you fall."

"Teamwork!" I say. "Leadership! Characters built of iron! Go, Parrots!"

Phil and Aysha do the commando course quickly and easily. Marco does it like a crazy monkey and falls off the tire bridge. Moppsy does it like a sleepy gorilla but doesn't fall off anything. Me? I try to do it like Phil and Aysha, but I slip off the log-climbing wall. But I cross the cable bridge, climb the rope net, and swing across the water like an expert.

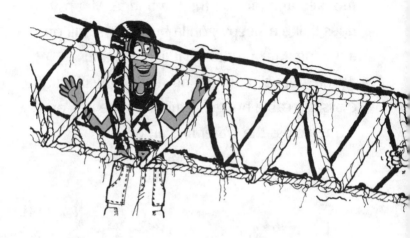

The other teams watch us. Someone from the Wolves yells out, "You Parrots have got no style! Look at your shoes, ya losers!"

I look at my sneakers. Yes, they have holes in them, but so what? Moppsy looks at Ms. Radcliff's old shoes. "Show them how it's done, Ms. R," he says. "Go wild!"

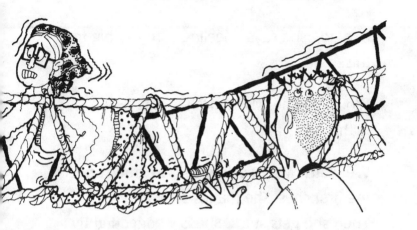

Ms. Radcliff doesn't look like she's about to go wild. She's got her red hair tied back under a scarf. She looks scared, but she steps up onto the cable bridge, with Aysha and me on either side.

"Just go steadily, Ms. R," Aysha says. "Hold on lightly and keep your balance right over your feet."

Ms. Radcliff does so and crosses the bridge beautifully. Now she has to crawl under a series of tightly crisscrossed branches.

"Oh no," she says kneeling. "I'm too big for this!"

"You'll be fine, Ms. Radcliff," I say. "Have faith."

We watch Ms. Radcliff begin to crawl under the branches. She makes slow progress. Then she gets stuck. She is wedged tightly under the lowest branches.

"I'm stuck!" she calls out. "Help!"

The other teams laugh.

"Don't worry," yells Moppsy. "Adrian and I will save you." And in we go—face to face with a trapped math teacher. Ms. Radcliff is puffing. And she has a muddy face, muddy hands, and muddy knees.

"I can see what the problem is," says
Moppsy. "It's the branches." And with that,
he arches his back and lifts the branches
right out of the way.

"You're free, Ms. Radcliff," I say. "Go, go, go!"

And go she does, covered in mud racing
stripes.

The Rolling River camp leader, whose name
is Jack McJock, calls all the "happy" campers
together.

"The Wolves team was the best on the
obstacle course," he says. "None of their
members got stuck anywhere or fell." Jack
McJock looks at us. "The Screaming Parrots
were the worst. They need to concentrate
more."

I shrug. We tried hard, and we tried to help each other. What else can a bunch of Parrots do? Jack McJock's words don't worry me, but they seem to have put Ms. Radcliff's back up.

"Oh, give me a break!" she mutters into her big hanky. "This isn't the army."

Jack McJock looks in our direction. His face is red and brown like a dried apple, and he's wearing a matching red and brown lumberjack's shirt. "I expect to see a better effort on the canoe and climbing course," he says.

Moppsy makes a beak with his two index fingers. "Parrot Power!" he yells. "We climb high, we paddle fast!"

I'm not sure that I know exactly what Mopps means, but I make the sign of the beak, too.

"Go, Parrots!" I say. "*Yarrrrrrk!*"

Chapter 4

Beaks of Steel!

We spend Tuesday and Wednesday roaming the woods and canoeing in calm water. On Thursday, the idea is to paddle up the Rolling River, climb up a cliff, then climb back down on ropes. Sounds easy enough, right?

The Screaming Parrots are doing quite well, I think—but Jack McJock doesn't agree. He sighs a lot when he sees us. "More *teamwork* is required here," he tells Ms. R loudly, "and more leadership. We are here to build *character*, Ms. Radcliff."

"Yes, Mr. Mc Jock," says Ms. R. "I'll try to do better."

Marco makes the sign of the beak. "Parrot team meeting," he whispers, "but no teachers." We put our heads together.

"OK," Marco says "we've got to take the heat off Ms. R. That Jack Mc Jock is out to get her. It's not her fault she's not a superwoman."

"Right," says Aysha. "I've heard she's terrified of rock climbing. We've got to make sure she feels safe."

"She doesn't like canoeing, either," says Moppsy.

"And I don't think she wants to come down the cliff on a rope," adds Phil.

"Well," I say, "she's helped me at school, so we'll help her tomorrow." I look around and see Ms. Radcliff sitting on a log. She doesn't look happy.

"I also think," says Aysha, "the Screaming Parrots have got to have some fun tomorrow. Don't let this Jack McJock scare us." She makes the sign of the beak. "Be strong, Parrots! Be strong!"

Chapter 5

Parrot Paddling Power

On Thursday morning, we pick our paddling partners for the trip upstream. We've decided that Moppsy will go with Ms. Radcliff because he's our best and strongest paddler.

"You and me, Ms. Radcliff!" Moppsy says. "We'll show these Wolves, Tigers, Warthogs, and Vultures how to do it."

Ms. Radcliff tries to smile. "I'm glad I've got my life jacket on," she says. "I'm not a great swimmer."

I hop into a canoe with Phil. Marco and Aysha get into another one. We're off!

Jack McJock watches us set out. "Stroke! Stroke! Stroke!" he yells. "You've got to beat that river!"

Adrian Swift does not want to *beat* the river. Man, I'm a surfer. I'm into nature. I want to make *friends* with the river.

"Paddle over this side, guys!" I call out. "The current's not as strong."

I see Ms. Radcliff is doing her best. She dips and pulls with her paddle and splashes Moppsy, but Moppsy doesn't say anything. He just powers the canoe along with his big arms.

"We're doing great!" I hear him say. "What a beautiful day!"

Moppsy's right. The sun is shining on us,
right down into the water. And the woods
are filled with birds. I'm enjoying this.

"What a place!" says Marco-man. "And the
good thing is old Jack McJock is a long way
back!"

Wrong! Here he comes in his little wooden
outboard motorboat. It sounds like an angry

mosquito. He circles us, rocking our canoes with waves, and then pulls into shore.

"Everything all right, Ms. Radcliff?" he calls.

"Oh, yes," she says, puffing. "How far to go still?"

Mr. McJock looks upstream. "Stop at the cliffs on the left-hand side." And then he turns his attention to the other canoe groups.

Chapter 6

Onward and Upward

We pull into shore below the cliffs. Around us, other groups are bringing in their canoes. My arms are tired, but I feel good.

"We," says Marco and points to the cliff "are going to climb *that?* How?"

Phil studies the crag of rock. "We'll be OK," he says. "There are plenty of holds to hang onto."

Where have I heard that before? I feel my hands getting sweaty already.

"I'm not really keen on heights," says Moppsy. "And those rocks really are *high.*"

Ms. Radcliff offers us a drink from her big water bottle. Her face is pink from her efforts in the canoe.

"Well, Mopps," she says, "if you're half as good at climbing as you are at paddling, you'll *fly* up there."

The rest of us Parrots join in.

"You'll do great, Mopps!"

"You've got muscle power, Mopps!"

"We'll look after you, Mopps!"

Moppsy smiles. "Do you guys really think I can do it?"

"Parrot-solutely!" says Marco. "Parrot-solutely!"

At Camp Rolling River, we've learned the basics of rock climbing. But apart from climbing a high, wooden wall, we haven't done any of the real stuff. Aysha and Phil, who know a lot about indoor rock climbing, can't wait to get started.

We let them go first. I hold one safety rope, Marco holds the other. Aysha and Phil move up the cliff steadily. Sometimes they call out to each other, suggesting good, safe holds. All of us Parrots, at the cliff bottom, look up.

"I never knew you kids were so talented," says Ms. Radcliff. "I'm really impressed."

Suddenly Jack McJock turns up, dressed like a mountaineer. He even has on a green hat with a big feather sticking out of it!

"You don't have to climb if you don't want to, Ms. Radcliff," he says. "We don't force people who are *really* scared."

I look at Ms. Radcliff. She pulls her shoulders back.

"I am scared, Mr. McJock," she says, "but I will certainly *try* to climb this cliff."

"Me, too," says Moppsy.

"Me, three," says Marco.

"Yo," I say.

Right—all of us will try to climb the cliff. This is the power of Parrot positive thinking.

"We've made it!" Aysha calls down. "Get Moppsy and Ms. Radcliff ready!"

Moppsy and Ms. Radcliff tie their safety ropes and put on helmets. Both look scared. I remember what I learned from Aysha and Phil when we climbed indoors at Belmore.

"Use your feet and legs," I say. "Rest when you can . . . go slowly . . . stay balanced."

As soon as Moppsy has climbed a short distance, he seems confident. He grasps the rock and steps up neatly. "Hey, this isn't so bad!" he calls out. "It's just like a ladder!"

Ms. Radcliff isn't doing so well. She seems to be stuck. She's not built like a rock climber. She's big and heavy, which makes going upward harder.

"Grit your teeth and do it!" Mr. McJock yells out. "Grit your teeth!"

What has gritting your teeth got to do with climbing a rock?

"Grab the next hold with both hands!" Phil calls out to her. "Then step up onto your right foot, Ms. Radcliff. Then rest."

Ms. Radcliff takes Phil's advice. Then she waves to us.

"I think I'll be OK now. But this is going to take a while."

That's all right—we've got all day!

Marco and I climb the cliff side by side. As we get higher we go slower, but we're having fun. The river looks like green glass from up here. I'm scared, but I'm happy.

"We're doing well!" I yell across to Marco.

"We're doing great!" he yells back at me.

And in a few minutes we are standing on top of the cliff above the river, above the woods and all the canoes.

Chapter 7

Down, Down, Down!

What goes up must come down. All of the Screaming Parrot team are standing on top of the cliff. And shortly all the Screaming Parrot team will climb over the cliff edge and lower ourselves down on ropes.

"If you can climb," says Aysha to everyone, "going down will be easy. Just do exactly what you were shown."

Lowering yourself on a rope is a lot different from climbing up a cliff tied to one. You walk down backward and control your speed by letting the rope slip.

We're actually quite a happy bunch of Screaming Parrots at the moment. We've all climbed the cliff. We think we can all get down it, too.

"Me and Ms. R first," says Moppsy. "We'll see how we do."

Ms. Radcliff and Mopps tie into their ropes and back over the cliff. Like many things, it sounds easy. It even looks easy, but is it? I don't know yet, but I guess I soon will.

Moppsy and Ms. R have made it down. It's Phil's and my turn now. Back toward the edge of the cliff I go. I can feel the big drop behind me. Phil calls out.

"Keep your feet against the cliff, Addy. Just take small steps—enjoy it!"

Enjoy it? That's easy for him to say. But after I've backed over the edge and got myself set, I feel OK. I let the rope slip a little way and slide downward. My feet are against solid rock. I haven't got far to go. I can hear the other Parrots.

"Looking good, Addy!"

"Take your time, man!"

"You're born to it, baby!"

And in a minute or so I'm on the riverbank, feeling proud of myself.

#
Radcliff to the Rescue

We Parrots set off downstream in our canoes. We certainly are a happy bunch. All of us have paddled a canoe, climbed up a cliff, and climbed back down. And not only are we pleased with ourselves, we're pleased with each other.

"This has been a really good day!" says Ms. Radcliff. "I was worried about the climbing, but I got through it—with a little bit of advice and help from my friends."

The Parrots are quiet. All I can hear is the gentle splashing of our paddles. It's not often a teacher calls you a friend, but on this trip, I guess that's what we all are.

"Yeah, it's been cool," says Phil. "We've had a ball."

"And it's not over yet," adds Aysha.

And boy, did she turn out to be right about that!

We pull our canoes up onto the sandy shore at Camp Rolling River and take out our backpacks. Around us all the other groups are doing the same. I can hear Jack McJock's boat buzzing around, and then he skims in and stops just out from shore. He keeps the motor going.

"You Parrots did a lot better today," he says. "I was pleased to see—"

Suddenly, there's a loud WHUMP!

Orange flames shiver and shake upward from Mr. McJock's boat. I hear him shout, and then I see him dive overboard. For one second, no one does anything. We just watch, too stunned to move.

"Quick, Parrots!" shouts Ms. Radcliff. "I'll need help!" And she runs past the canoes and into the water.

Ms. R wades out. We follow her until she turns and yells, "Make a chain! Hold hands, everyone . . . all the way back to shore!"

Kids and leaders come from everywhere to form a human chain, but it's Ms. Radcliff who's out near the burning boat. She's up to her ribs in water. And then she does an amazing thing.

She dives, disappears, then comes up under the boat's bow. And now she's pushing the burning boat away from Mr. McJock. Above her there's smoke and fire, but she doesn't stop. She swims, pushing the boat away, then she gives it a shove, sending it even farther out from shore. Now she swims back to Mr. McJock, who is struggling.

By this time the human chain is walking its way out through the water, with big Moppsy up front, his hand out.

"Here we come, Ms. R!" he calls. "Get ready!"

"Hold tight, everyone!" Marco is shouting. "Grip hard! We can do this!"

I'm in the middle of the chain, and I get the feeling there's no way anyone will let anybody else go. We're all solidly locked and linked together.

Ms. Radcliff is dragging Mr. McJock back through the water. Her hair has fallen down from the top of her head and she's lost her glasses, but she's not slowing down. Moppsy puts out his hand to help, and now he has hold of Ms. R's hand. And then we all walk back to shore in one long, strong line, dragging Mr. McJock. *Fantastic!*

On Friday morning, as the bus pulls out of Camp Rolling River, the Screaming Parrots are again in the backseat. I turn to watch the river and the old wooden huts slide from sight. Man, what a week!

"Well," I say to Ms. Radcliff, "we might not have had the snazziest shoes in the place, but we had the best leader."

"Thank you, Adrian," she says, "but a leader is really only as good as his or her team. And you guys made a great team."

"And since we've all got great *character*," says Moppsy, "we've achieved Parrot-solutely *everything* we were supposed to."

"And more," says Marco. "And more."

"Next question is," says Aysha, "will there be any waves in Blue Water Bay this weekend?"

"High tide Saturday morning," says Marco.

"Sunny weather for sure," says Mopps.

"Looks like an offshore wind," says Phil.

So although I'm no mathematical genius, it all adds up. There'll be big surf in Blue Water Bay tomorrow, and we'll be there!

"Let the adventure begin!" I shout. "Again!"

About the Author

David Metzenthen

David Metzenthen tries really hard to write books that most definitely could be true! He is interested in sailboarding, indoor rock climbing, fishing, the environment, and good books. He is married and has two children and a goldfish called George, who eats like a horse.

David likes to write stories that contain action, adventure, and ideas about life. He hopes that his stories and characters will find a place in your memory, as well as on your bookshelf.

About the Illustrator

Michelle Ker

Michelle Ker lives in a big, old rambling house with a dog, a cat, and some nosy neighbors who think she is odd and wonder what she does all day in that room under the house.

Michelle loves music and plays drums. She gets a lot of the ideas for how characters look from watching rock bands.

She does all kinds of drawings for all kinds of people, but she likes drawing for kids' books the best. The characters have more fun, do mischievous things, and have better hairdos than people in other kinds of books.